SCHIRMER'S LIBRARY
OF MUSICAL CLASSICS

T0061302

ROBERT SCHUMANN

Vocal Album

Fifty-Five Songs with
Piano Accompaniment

English Translations by
DR. THEODORE BAKER

For HIGH VOICE — Library Vol. 120

→ For LOW VOICE — Library Vol. 121

G. SCHIRMER, Inc.

DISTRIBUTED BY

HAL•LEONARD®
CORPORATION
7777 W. BLUEMOUND RD. P.O. BOX 13819 MILWAUKEE, WI 53213

CONTENTS

FIFTY - FIVE SONGS

„Lieb' Liebchen, leg's Händchen."

"Dear love, lay thy hand."

(H. Heine.)

English version by Dr. Th. Baker.

Composed 1840.
Op. 24, Nº 4.

Nicht schnell.
Moderato.

1.

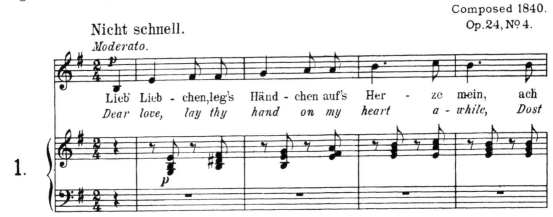

Lieb' Lieb - chen, leg's Händ - chen auf's Her - ze mein, ach
Dear love, lay thy hand on my heart a - while, Dost

hörst du, wie's po - chet im Käm - mer - lein? Da hau - set ein
hear in its cham - ber the ham - mer toil? With - in is a

Zim - mer - mann schlimm und arg, der zim - mert mir ei - nen
car - pen - ter grim and dark, And there on my cof - fin

12873

Printed in the U.S.A.

Tod - ten - sarg.
he's at work.

Es häm - mert und
He's hamm - 'ring and

klo - pfet bei Tag und bei Nacht, es hat mich schon längst um den
pound - ing all day and all night, And long he has robb'd me of

Schlaf ge - bracht. Ach spu - tet euch, Mei ster Zim - mer -
slum - ber's right; Sir Car - pen - ter, let your ham - mer

mann, da - mit ich bal - de schla - fen kann.
leap, For soon I'd glad - ly fall a - sleep.

„Schöne Wiege meiner Leiden.“

"Lovely cradle of my sorrow."

English version by Dr. Th. Baker.   (Heine.)   Composed 1840.
Op. 24, N°5.

wo - da wan - delt Lieb - chen traut, le - be wohl, du
Hal-low'd by my dar - -ling's feet, Fare thee well, thou

heil' - ge Stel - le, wo ich sie zu-erst geschaut. Le - be
spot e'er ho - ly, Where at first we train did meet. Fare thee

Rascher.
Più mosso.

wohl, le - be wohl. Hätt' ich dich doch nie ge-seh'n, schöne Her - zens -
well, fare thee well. Would that I had nev - er seen thee. Of my heart the

kö - ni - gin! nim - mer, nim - mer wär' es dann gesche - hen, dass ich
love - ly queen! Nev - er, nev - er had I thought to win thee, Nor had

jetzt so e - lend bin.___
er - er know this pain.___

Nie wollt' ich dein Her - ze rühren,
I have nev - er___ sought___ thy fa - vor,
Lie - be hab' ich

nie ___ er-fleht;
heart ___ to me;
nur ein stil - les Le - be füh - ren
'Twas my low - ly heart's en - deav - or

wollt' ich, wo dein O - dem weht,
On - ly to be near to thee,
wo dein O - dem weht. Doch du
on - ly near___ to thee. Yet thy

drängst mich selbst von hinnen, bitt'- re Wor - te spricht dein Mund; Wahn - sinn
lip my doom pronounces, Bids me harsh- ly to de- part, Mad - ness

wühlt in meinen Sin - nen. und mein Herz ist krank___ und wund.
burns in all my sens- es, And I'm ill and sore___ at heart.

Und die Glie - - der. matt und trä - ge, schlepp' ich,
And with trem - bling limbs o - -bey - -ing, Slow - ly,

schlepp' ich fort am Wan - der- stab,___ bis mein mü - des Haupt'ich
slow ly forth from thee___ I stray,___ Till my wea - ry head be

„Mit Myrthen und Rosen."

"With Myrtle and Roses."

(H. Heine.)

English version by Dr. Th. Baker.

Composed 1840.
Op. 24, No 9.

sar-gen mei - ne Lieder hinein. O könnt'ich die Liebe sar-gen hin-zu!
there my songs to rest I would lay. Oh, could I but lay my love there-un-to!

Auf dem Gra-be der Lie-be wüchst Blümlein der Ruh', da
On the grave of my love there are flow-ers of rue; So

blüht es her-vor, da pflückt man es ab, doch mir blüht's nur, wenn ich
fair-ly it blooms, they ga-ther it yon; For me 'twill bloom on my

sel - ber im Grab, wenn ich sel - ber im Grab.
own grave a-lone, on my own grave a-lone.

Hier sind nun die Lie-der, die
Now these are the songs that of

einst   so wild   wie ein   La - va - strom, der dem Aet - na entquillt,   her-
yore   were wild   As e'er   la - va - stream, when from Æt - na it boil'd;   They

vor — ge-stürzt aus   dem tief - sten Ge-müth und rings viel   bli - tzen - de
pour'd   a-main from   the heart's foun-tain-head, And sparks flew   flash-ing where

Fun - ken   ver-sprüht. Nun   lie - gen sie stumm   und   tod - ten-gleich, nun
on - ward   they sped. They   now   lie so mute,   so   dead they seem   And

12

12878

Widmung.
Dedication.

English version by Dr. Th. Baker.   (Fr. Rückert.)

"Myrthen", Op. 25; No. 1.
Composed 1840.

Innig, lebhaft.
Con affetto; animato.

4.

Du mei-ne See - le, du mein
Thou art my soul, and thou my

Herz,   du mei-ne Wonn',   o du mein
heart,   Thou all my joy   and sor - row

Schmerz,   du mei-ne Welt,   in der ich le - be, mein Him - mel
art,   Thou art my world   for life a - dor - ing, My heav'n art

du,   da - rein ich schwe - be, o du mein Grab,   in das hin -
thou   where-in I'm soar - ing; O thou my grave,   where-in for

12873

a tempo ... ritard.

lie - bend ü - ber mich, mein gu - ter Geist, mein bess'res
love doth lift me high, My guar - dian fay, my bet - ter

a tempo ... ritard.

Ich!
I!

a tempo

Du mei-ne See - le, du mein Herz, du mei-ne
Thou art my soul, and thou my heart, Thou all my

a tempo

Wonn', o du mein Schmerz, du mei-ne Welt, in der ich
joy and sor-row art, Thou art my world for life a-

le - be, mein Him - mel du, da - rein ich schwe - be, mein gu - ter
dor - ing, My heav'n art thou, where - in I'm soar - ing, My guardian

Geist, mein bess'-res Ich!
fay, my bet - ter I!

Der Nussbaum.

The Nut-tree.

(Julius Mosen.)

English version by Dr. Th. Baker.

"Myrthen," Op. 25; No 3.
Composed 1840.

Es
There

grü - net ein Nuss - - baum vor dem Haus,
stands a green nut - - tree near yon door,

duf - tig, luf - tig
Rare - ly, Air - i - ly

breit - tet er blätt'- rig die Blät - ter aus.
Spread - ing its leaf - y ar - ray be - fore,

fahn.
blow.

Es
The

flü - stern je zwei und zwei ge-paart,
blos - soms are whis - p'ring two by two;

nei - gend, beu - gend zier - lich zum
Wend - ing, Bend - ing, Ten - der - ly

Kus - se die Häupt - chen zart.
kiss - ing, their heads they bow.

riten.

Licht,   und ihm ent-schlei-ert sie freund-lich ihr
lure,   To him she glad-ly un-veil-eth Her

a poco a poco
nach und nach

from-mes Blu-men-ge-sicht.   Sie blüht und glüht und
snow-white flow-er-face pure.   She blooms, and glows, and

accel.
schneller — — — — — — — —

leuch-tet,   und star-ret stumm in die Höh',____ sie
light-ens,   And gaz-es mute-ly on high,____ Ex-

— — — — — — — *rit.* p

duf-tet und wei-net und zit-tert   vor Lie-be und Lie-bes-
hal-ing and weep-ing and trembling   rit.   For love and love's o-ver-

rit. — — —

weh,   vor Lie-be und Lie-bes-weh.
joy,   for love and love's o-ver-joy.

rit.

„Was will die einsame Thräne?"

"What will this tear so lonely?"

(H. Heine.)

English version by Dr. Th. Baker.

"Myrthen", Op. 25; No. 21.
Composed 1840.

Ziemlich langsam, mit inniger Empfindung.
Piuttosto lento, con molto affetto.

12873

„Du bist wie eine Blume."

"Ah, sweet as any flower."

(H. Heine.)

English version by Dr. Th. Baker.

Composed 1840.
Op. 25, No 24.

„Dem rothen Röslein gleicht mein Lieb'."

"A red, red rose."

(R. Burns.)

Composed 1840.
Op.27, Nº 2.

9.

f

Meer! Und wür - den tro - cken Strom und Meer, und schmöl - zen Fels und
dry. Till a' the seas gang dry, my dear; And the rocks melt wi' the

p

Stein, _____ ich wür-de den-noch le - benslang Dir Herz und See - le
sun: _____ (yet) I — will love thee still, my dear, While the sands of life shall

ritard.

weih'n! Nun, hol - des Liebchen, le - be wohl! leb' wohl, du süs-se Maid!
run. And fare thee well, my on - ly love! And fare thee well a - while! And

a tempo

Bald kehr' ich wie - der, wär' ich auch zehn - tau-send Mei - len weit!
I — will come a - gain, my luve, Tho' it were ten thou - sand mile!

Der Hidalgo.

The Hidalgo.

(E. Geibel.)

Op. 30, Nº 3.
Composed 1840.

English version by Lewis Novra.

Schim - mer, da treibt's mich fort vom Zim - mer, durch
bright - ly, We seek ad - ven - tures night - ly In

Platz und Gas - sen weit; da bin zur Lieb' ich
street or gar - den gay! And sing and laugh as

im - mer wie zum Ge - fecht, wie zum Ge - fecht be - reit.
light - ly When hearts or foes, when hearts or foes we slay!

Es ist so süss zu scher - zen mit Lie - dern und mit
We live 'mid strife and court - ing, With hearts we're ev - er

34

36

12873

sin - - ge, die Zi - - - ther und die
we go, A sword of keen To -
Klin - ge vom To - - le - dan'-schen Stahl. Ich
le - do, Each car- - ries at his side, Our
p
sf
sing' an man-chem Git - ter und höh - - ne man-chen
jo - - vial songs re - sound-ing, With mer - - ry jests a -
Rit - ter mit ke-ckem Lied zu - mal; den
bound-ing, Our ri - vals all de - ride; Whose
f

stun - den, sie brin - - gen Lie - bes - kun - den, sie
hours ___ When Love dis-plays his pow - ers, And

brin - - - gen blut' - gen Strauss, und Blu - men o - der
dead - - ly pas - sions reign; Be - deck'd with wounds or

Wun - - den trag' mor - - gen ich nach Haus.
flow - ers At morn we'll home a - gain.

Auf denn zum A - ben - teu - er, schon losch der Son - ne
A - way, the sun's de - clin - ing, The moon is faint - ly

Die Löwenbraut.
The Lion's Bride.
(A. v. Chamisso.)

English version by Dr. Th. Baker.

Op. 31, № 1.
Composed 1840.

Mit der
With the

Myr - the ge-schmückt und dem Braut - ge-schmeid, des Wär - ters Toch - ter, die
myr - tle a - dorn'd as a bride ar - ray'd, The keep - er's daugh-ter, the

ro - si - ge Maid, tritt ein in den Zwin - ger des Lö - wen; er liegt der
ros - y maid, Steps in - to the cage of the li - on; he lies Be -

Etwas langsamer.
Poco più lento.

„Wir wa - ren in Ta - gen, die nicht mehr
"In days that will nev - er re - turn a -

sind, gar treu - e Ge-spie - len wie Kind und Kind, und
gain, How art-less we play'd, like two chil - dren then; Our

hat - ten uns lieb und hat - ten uns gern; die Ta - ge der Kind-heit, sie lie - gen uns
hearts were so fond, our hearts were so kind: The days of our child-hood now lie far be -

fern. Du schüt-tel-test macht-voll, eh' wir's ge - glaubt, dein
hind. For ere we had thought, thy mane was dis - play'd Right

mäh-ne-um-wog-tes kö-nig-lich Haupt; ich wuchs her-an, du siehst es: ich
roy-al in pow'r, o'er-mantling thy head; I grew, as well, for thou dost be-

bin,— ich bin das Kind nicht mehr mit kin-di-schem Sinn. O
hold No more the child, the child thou knew-est of old. O

wär' ich das Kind noch und blie-be bei dir, mein
were I a child still to stay here with thee, Thou

star-kes, ge-treu-es, mein red-li-ches Thier! Ich
strong, faith-ful friend, ev-er loy-al to me! But

Thrä - nen nicht die Bli - cke mehr hell.___ Ver -
tears mine eyes for ev - er be - dim.___ Dost

stehst du mich ganz? Schaust grim - mig da - zu, ich
hear me a - right? How grim is thine eye! My

bin ja ge - fasst, sei ru - hig auch du; dort seh' ihn ihn kommen, dem fol - gen ich
fears I have quell'd, be calm, then, as I.___ But yon-der he's com-ing, who now calls me

muss, so geb' ich denn, Freund, dir den letz - ten Kuss!"
his: So, friend, let me give thee a fare-well kiss!"

Tempo I.

mf

p *ritard.*

p *pp*

wie ihn die Lip - pe des Mäd-chens be - rührt, da hat man den Zwin - ger er -
hard - ly the lip of the maid he doth feel, The bars that im - pound him all

Und
And

a tempo

mf

zit - tern ge - spürt, und wie er am Zwin - ger den Jüng - ling er - schaut, er -
trem - ble and reel; And when he be - yond of the bride - groom is 'ware, The

fasst Ent - set - zen die ban - gen - de Braut. Er
maid - en thrills with a fear - ful de - spair! He

f

f

stellt an die Thür sich des Zwin-gers zur Wacht, er schwin-get den Schweif, er
stands as on guard by the door of the cage, He lash-es his flanks, he

brül-let mit Macht; sie fle-hend, ge-bie-tend und dro-hend be-gehrt hin-aus;
roars in his rage: Im-plor-ing, com-mand-ing and threat'ning she fain Would forth:

er im Zorn den Aus-gang wehrt.
he doth fierce the door main-tain.

Und draussen er-hebt sich verwor-ren Ge-schrei. Der
Out-side there a-ris-es a cry of a-larm. The

48

Jüng-ling ruft: bringt Waf-fen her-bei, ich schiess' ihn nie-der, ich treff' ihn gut.
bride-groom calls:"Bring hith-er an arm! One shot will kill him, if e'er I fire!"

Auf-brüllt der Ge-reiz-te, schäumend vor Wuth. Die Un-se-li-ge wagt's sich, der
Wild rag-es the li-on, foam-ing in ire. In dis-may she en-deav-ors the

Thü-re zu nah'n, da fällt er ver-wan-delt die Her-rin an: die
door-way to gain But on her in fu-ry he falls a-main: And

schö-ne Ge-stalt, ein gräss-li-cher Raub, liegt blu-tig zer-ris-sen ent-stellt in dem Staub.
ghast-ly her form, so charm-ful be-fore, Lies gor-y and torn in the grime on the floor.

Und wie er vergos-sen das
And there, af-ter spilling that

theu - re Blut, er legt sich zur Lei - che mit fin - ste - rem Muth, er
dear life - blood, He lies by the corpse in a grim, sul - len mood; He

liegt so ver - sun - ken in Trau - er und Schmerz, bis tödt - lich die Ku - gel ihn
dreams in his pain and his sor - row a - part, Till dead - ly the ball speeds a-

trifft in das Herz.
way to his heart.

Adagio.

Wanderlied.
The Farewell.
(Kerner.)

Composed 1840.
Op.35, No 3.

Sehr lebhaft.
Vivacissimo.

12.

Wohl - auf! noch getrun - ken den
Come, fill up a bum-per be-

fun - kelnden Wein! A - de nun, ihr Lie - ben, ge - schie-den muss sein. A -
fore we de-part, A - gain will I pledge ye, old friends of my heart! Fare-

de nun, ihr Ber - ge, du vä - ter-lich Haus! Es treibt in die Fer - ne mich
well, love-ly scenes, dear to kin-dred and home, For leave ye I must, through the

mäch - tig hinaus! Die
wide world to roam. The

12873

Son-ne, sie blei bet am Him-mel nicht stehn, es treibt sie durch Län - der und
sun in the heav-ens he nev - er stands still, But rolls in his or - bit his

Mee - re zu gehn, die Wo - ge nicht haf - tet am ein - sa-men Strand, die
course to ful-fil: The bil - lows re - tire from the wide-spreading sand, The

Stür - me, sie brau - sen mit Macht durch das Land!
storm in its might rush-es o - ver the land.

Mit ei - len - den Wol - ken der Vo - gel dort zieht und
The bird with the cloud wing-eth swift-ly a - way, And

singt in der Fer - ne ein hei - mathlich Lied. So treibt es den Bur - schen durch
sings in a far land her old,— hap-py lay. *And youth full of ar - dor leaves*

Etwas langsamer.
Poco più lento.

ritard. *a tempo*

Wälder und Feld, zu gleichen der Mut-ter, der wan-dernden Welt!
all it holds dear, Re - joicing in change, like this wan - der-ing sphere.

Da grü - ssen ihn Vö - gel be - kannt ü - berm Meer, sie
In lands o'er the o - cean the for - est sup-plies The

flo - gen von Flu - ren der Hei-math hier - her, da duf - ten die Blu - men ver-
birds that so oft - en at home met his eyes, While flow'rs in their beau - ty a-

trau-lich um ihn, sie trie - ben vom Lan - de die Lüf - te da-hin. Die
dorn all the ground, And fill with their o - dor the val - leys a-round. The

ri-tar-

Vö - gel, die ken - nen sein vä - terlich Haus,   die Blu - men, die pflanzt' er der
song - sters remind him of home by their lay;   The flow'rs, of his dear one in

dan - do   ri - tar - dan - do

Lie - be zum Strauss, und Lie - be, die folgt ihm, sie geht ihm zur Hand: so
gar - lands of May, And love nev - er leaves him, wher - e'er he may roam, But

dan - do

ri - tar - dan - do

a tempo   ritard.

wird ihm zur Hei - math das fer - ne - ste Land,   so wird ihm zur Hei - math das
far a - mong stran - gers he still is at home,   But far a - mong stran - gers he

a tempo   ritard.

Tempo I.

f

fer - neste Land.
still is at home.

Wohl - auf! noch getrunken den
Come, fill up a bum - per be -

fun - kelnden Wein! A - de nun, ihr Lie - ben, ge - schie - den muss sein.   A -
fore we de - part, A - gain will I pledge ye, old friends of my heart!   Fare -

p

Ped.   Ped.

Erstes Grün.

Earliest Green.

(Justinus Kerner.)

English version by Dr. Th. Baker.

Composed 1840.
Op. 35, No. 4.

Du jun - ges Grün, du fri - sches Gras! wie
Thou ear - ly green, thou smil - ing field! How

man - ches Herz durch dich ge - nas, das von des Win - ters
man - ya heart thy sight has heal'd, Ill ev - er win - ter

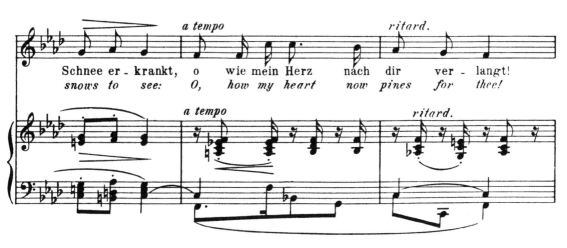

Schnee er - krankt, o wie mein Herz nach dir ver - langt!
snows to see: O, how my heart now pines for thee!

Schon wächst du aus der Er - de Nacht, wie dir mein Herz ent -
From night - ly sleep where thou hast lain, Dost greet my joy - ful

ge - gen lacht! Hier in des Wal - des stil - lem Grund drück' ich dich, Grün, an
eye a - gain, Here in the wood-land lone - li - ness Thee to my heart, my

Herz und Mund.
lips I press.

Wie treibt's mich von den Men- schen fort! Mein
How fain am I from men to go! No

Leid, das hebt kein Men- schenwort, nur jun - ges Grün, an's Herz gelegt,
mor - tal word can still my wo; Fresh green a-lone, laid on___ my breast,

macht, dass mein Her - ze stil - ler schlägt.
Can ev - er soothe my heart's un-rest.

Stille Thränen.
Hidden Tears.

English version by Dr. Th. Baker.   (Justinus Kerner.)

Composed 1840.
Op. 35, № 10.

14.

Du bist ___ vom Schlaf _ er -stan - den
By slum - ber now__ for-sak - en,

und wan - delst durch ___ die Au', _____ da
Thou wan - d'rest o'er_____ the mead, _____ Wher-

liegt ___ ob al - len Lan - den _____ der Him - mel
e'er ___ thy way ___ be tak - en _____ Blue skies ___ are

wun - der-blau. ___ So lang ___ du oh - ne
calm - ly spread. ___ While thou ___ un - heed - ful

12873

man - cher aus ____ den Schmerz, ____ und
tears ____ from eyes ____ full sad, ____ And

mor - gens dann ____ ihr mei - net, ____
then ____ ye think, ____ at morn - ing,

stets fröh - lich sei ____ sein Herz;
Their hearts are al - - - ways glad,

Sonntags am Rhein.

Sunday on the Rhine.

(Reinick.)

English version by
Dr. Th. Baker.

Composed 1840.
Op.36, Nº1.

Mässig geschwind.

Moderato. *p*

15.

Des Sonn - tag's in der Mor - genstund' wie wan-dert's sich so
How sweet it is on Sun - day morn To stray a - long the

schön am Rhein, wennrings in wei - ter Rund' die Mor - genglo - cken
Rhine, When ear - ly chimes, on breez - es borne, From far and near com -

geh'n! Ein Schiff - lein zieht auf blau - er Fluth, da singt's und ju - belt's
bine! There glides a boat o'er a - zure flood, And joy - ful songs re -

d'rein; Du Schiff - lein, gelt, das fährt sich gut in all' die Lust hin - ein? Vom
sound; O say, thou boat, is gay thy mood Where all is gay a - round? From

Dor - fe hal - let Or - gelton, es tönt ein frommes Lied, an -
yon - derchurch the or - gan-peal With songs of wor-ship blends, While

däch - tig dort die Pro - cession aus der__ Ca - pel - le zieht. Und
slow a throng pro - ces - sional From out__ the doorway wends. And,

ernst in all' die Herr - lichkeit die Burg hernie - der schaut, und
grave against the smil - ing sky, Looks down yon cas - tle - tow'r,__ That

spricht von al - ter gu - terZeit, die auf__ den Fels ge - baut.__
tells of good old times gone by, When found - ed was its pow'r.

Das Al - les beut der präch' - geRhein an sei - nem Re - ben -
All these doth Fa - ther Rhine display A - long his vine-clad

strand, und spie-gelt recht im hell-sten Schein das gan-ze Va-ter-
strand, And mir-rors, on his shin-ing way, The broad-er Fa-ther-

land, das from-me treu-e Va-terland in sei-ner vol-len
land; The true, de-vot-ed Fa-therland In all its splen-dor

Pracht, mit Lust und Lie-dern al-lerhand vom lie-ben Gott be-dacht.
shows, With joy and song on ev-ry hand, That our dear Lord be-stows.

An den Sonnenschein.

"O shining sun."

English version by
Dr. Th. Baker.

(Reinick.)

Composed 1840.
Op. 36. No. 4.

16.

O Sonnenschein, o Sonnenschein! wie scheinst du mir in's Herz hinein, weckst
O shining sun, O shining sun, Thy bright-ness all my heart has won, And

drin - nen lau - ter Lie-bes-lust, dass mir so en - ge wird die Brust.
thoughts of love thou waken-est, That all too nar-row grows my breast.

Und en - ge wird mir Stub' und Haus, und
Too nar-row are my house and home, And

wenn ich lauf' zum Thor hin - aus, da lockst du gar in's fri-sche Grün die
when I thro' the gate-way roam, Thou lur-est on, a - mid the green, The

al - lerschönsten Mädchen hin, die al - lerschönsten Mäd - chen!
fair-est maidens all, I ween, the fair-est all of mai - dens!

O Sonnenschein, du glau-best wohl, dass ich wie du es ma-chen soll, der
O shining sun, dost think of me, That I shall dare to do like thee? Who

je - de schmucke Blu-me küsst, die e - ben nur sich dir er-schliesst. Hast
kiss-est ev - 'ry pret-ty flow'r That o-pens on - ly to thy pow'r. Yet

doch so lang die Welt er-blickt, und weisst, das sich's für mich nicht schickt;
thou hast seen the world so long, And well dost know, for me 'twere wrong!

Was machst du mir denn sol - che Pein? O Son-nenschein, o Son-nenschein!
Then why hast thou my heart un-done? O shin-ing sun, O shin-ing sun!

Intermezzo.

"Thine image pure."

(Eichendorff.)

Composed 1840,
Op.39, № 2.

Waldesgespräch.

Loreley.

(Eichendorff.)

English version by Dr. Th. Baker.

Composed 1840.
Op.39. №3.

Ziemlich rasch.
Vivace.

18.

spät, es ist schon kalt, was reit'st du ein - - sam durch den
late, the night is cold, Why rid'st thou lone - - ly thro' the

Wald? Der Wald ist lang, du bist al - lein, du schö - ne Braut.ich führ dich
wold? The way is long, thou art a - lone, Thou lore-ly bride, O be_ mine

heim!" Gross ist der Män - ner Trug____ und
own!" Great is the guile - ful art____ of

12873

List, vor Schmerz mein Herz ge - bro - chen ist;
men, *My heart with - in me breaks for pain:*

wohl irrt das Wald-horn her und hin, o flieh', o
Hark! how the horn winds low and dim, Oh flee, oh

flieh', du weisst nicht, wer ich bin! „So reich ge - schmückt ist
flee, thou knows't not who I am!" "So gay thy steed, so

Ross und Weib, so wun - der-schön, so wun - der-schön der jun - ge
rare thy charm, So won-drous fair, so wondrous fair thy youth - ful

ritard. f a tempo f ritard.

Leib; jetzt kenn' ich dich, Gott steh' mir bei, du bist die He - xe Lo - re -
form: I know thee now, God be my stay! Thou art the de-mon Lo - re -
ritard. a tempo ritard.

12873

Die Stille.
Silence.

(Eichendorff.)

English version by Dr. Th. Baker.

Composed 1840.
Op.39. N? 4.

Mondnacht.
By Moonlight.

English version by Dr. Th. Baker.

(Eichendorff.)

Composed 1840.
Op.39, Nº 5.

Und mei - ne See - - le spann - te
And my rapt soul ___ her pin - ions

a tempo

weit ih - re Flü - gel aus,
In ea - ger joy out - spread,

ritard. a tempo

flog durch die stil - len Lan - de, als
And o - ver Earth's do - min - ions As

flö - ge ___ sie nach Haus. ___
home - ward ___ on she sped. ___

p

pp

Im Walde.

In the Forest.

(J. von Eichendorff.)

English version by Dr. Th. Baker.

Composed 1840.
Op. 39, Nº 11.

Es zog ei - ne Hoch-zeit den Berg ent-lang,
There pass'd on the moun-tain a wed-ding train,

ich
The

hör - te die Vö - gel schla-gen,
birds were all warbling loud - ly,

da
And

blitz-ten viel Rei-ter, das Waldhorn klang,
das
glit-ter-ing rid-ers dash'd on a - main,
Their

war ein lus-ti-ges Ja - gen!
horns resounding so proud-ly!

Und eh' ich's ge-dacht, war al - les ver-hallt,
And ere I had thought, 'twas still all a-round, a tempo

die Nacht be-de-cket die
In night all na-ture was

Frühlingsnacht.
Spring Night.

English version by Dr. Th. Baker.

(Eichendorff.)

Composed·1840.
C.ₚ.39, N⁰ 12.

Ziemlich rasch. Leidenschaftlich.

22.

12873

Trau — me rauscht's — der Hain, und die
dream — y grove — doth join, *And the*

Nach - ti - gal - len schla-gen's: "Sie ist Dei — ne, sie ist
night - in - gales all tell it: *"She is thine! — ah! she is*

Dein!" (Words of 2d Verse by Lie-bes-
thine!" R. Pohl.) *All of*

Früh — ling, mir — im Her — zen,
love and Spring - time glad — ness

blü — — het auf in vol - ler Pracht, und der
Fills my bo - som with de - light! *And the*

„Seit ich ihn gesehen."
"Since mine eyes have seen him."

(Chamisso.)

Composed 1840.
Op.42, № 1.

12873

„Er, der Herrlichste von Allen."

"He, the best of all."

(Chamisso.)

Composed 1840.
Op. 42, Nº 2.

Wahl. _____ und ich will die Ho - he seg-nen vie-le tau - - send-
be, _____ And a thou-sand times I'll bless her, who is thus_____ be-lov'd by

mal; wil mich freu-en dann und wei - nen, se - lig, se-lig bin ich
thee. Shedding tears, al-tho' re - joic - ing, hap - py, happy then my

dann, _____ soll-te mir das Herz auch bre-chen, brich, o Herz, was liegt _____ dar-
lot: _____ E'en tho' my poor heart be bro-ken, break, O heart, it mat - - ters

an?
not.

a tempo

„Ich kann's nicht fassen, nicht glauben.

English version by
Dr. Th. Baker.

"I can not, dare not believe it."

(Chamisso.)

Composed 1840.
Op. 42, No 3.

Mit Leidenschaft.
Con passione.

25.

Ich kann's nicht fas-sen, nicht glau-ben, es hat ein Traum mich be-
I can not, dare not be-lieve it, Ah, sure-ly, 'tis but a

rückt,___ wie hätt' er doch un-ter Al-len mich Ar-me er-
dream,___ For why should poor I be cho-sen, Be blest and ex-

Etwas langsamer.
Poco più lento.

höht und be-glückt? Mir war's, er ha-be ge-spro-chen: ..ich
alt-ed by him? Me-seems as if he had spo-ken: "I

bin auf e-wig dein,___ mir war's ich träu-me noch im-mer.
am for-ev-er thine!"___ Me-seems as were I still dream-ing.

ritard.

a tempo

12873

es hat ein Traum mich be - - rückt.___ wie hätt' er doch un - ter
Ah, sure - ly, 'tis but a dream,___ For why should poor I be

Al - len mich Ar-me er - höht und be - glückt?
cho - sen, Be blest and ex - alt - ed by him?

Ich kann's nicht fas-sen, nicht glau -
I can not, dare not be - - lieve

ben, es hat ein Traum mich be - rückt.___
it, ah, sure - ly, 'tis but a dream!___

Der Ring.

The Ring.

(Chamisso.)

Composed 1840.
Op.42, No 4.

Innig.
Con molto affetto.

Du Ring an mei-nem Fin- -ger, mein gol-de-nes Rin-ge-
Thou ring up-on my fin- -ger, My beau-ti-ful ring of

lein, ich_ drü-cke dich fromm an die Lip- -pen, dich
gold, My_ lips on thee fer-vent-ly lin- -ger, And

fromm an die Lip-pen, an das Her- -ze mein. Ich hatt' ihn aus- -ge-
close the dear treasure to my heart I hold'. My child-hood's dream had

träu- -met, der Kind-heit fried-lich schö-nen Traum, ich
van- -ish'd, A joy-ous dream_ se-rene and bright; A-

fand al-lein mich ver - lo - ren im ö - den, un-end - li-chen
lone I seem'd as if ban-ish'd To des - o - late re - gious of

Raum. Du Ring an mei - - nem Fin - - ger, da
night. Thou ring up - on my fin - ger, Hast

hast du mich erst be - lehrt, hast mei - nem Blick er-
giv'n to glad thougths a birth, For - bid - dest clouds to

poco
nach

schlos - sen des Le - bens un-end - li-chen, tie - fen Werth. Ich
lin - ger, Trans - form - est to rap - ture my life on earth, And

a poco accelerando
und nach rascher

will ihm die-nen, ihm le - ben, ihm an - ge-hö - ren
I'll live for him and near him, Will al - - ways his re -

12873

ganz, hin sel - ber mich ge - ben und fin - den ver-klärt mich, und
main, To serve him, to bless and to cheer him, His glance of ap -

fin - den ver-klärt mich in sei - nem Glanz. Du Ring an mei - nem
pro-val to gain, his ap - pro-val gain. Thou ring up-on my

Fin - - ger, mein gol-de-nes Rin - ge-lein, ich drü-cke dich fromm an die
fin - - ger, My beau-ti-ful ring of gold, My lips on thee fer-vent-ly

Lip - - pen, dich fromm an die Lip-pen, an das Her - - ze mein!
lin - - ger, And close the dear treasure to my heart I hold!

„Helft mir, ihr Schwestern."

"Help me, oh sisters."

(A. von Chamisso.)

English version by Dr. Th. Baker.

Composed 1840.
Op.42, № 5.

Ziemlich schnell.
Piuttosto allegro.

Helft mir, ihr Schwes-tern,
Help me, oh sis - ters,

27.

Immer mit Pedal.
Sempre con Pedale

freund-lich mich schmü - cken, dient_ der Glück-li-chen heu — te, mir.
fond-ly a-dorn me, Deck_ to-day the re - joic - ing bride,

Win - det ge-schäf - tig mir um die Stir - ne noch_ der blü-hen-den
*Light-ly en-twine ye o - ver my fore - head Now_ the bloom-ing_*

Myr - the Zier. Als ich be-frie - digt, freu - di-gen Her - zens,
myr - tle's pride. While so con-tent - ed, so hap-py-heart - ed,

12873

sonst dem Ge-lieb-ten im Ar - me lag, im-mer noch rief er,
Else in the arms of my love__ I lay, Still he would sigh, with

Sehn-sucht im Her - zen, un - ge-dul - dig den heu - ti-gen Tag.
heart full of long-ing, Fain to hast - en this tar - dy day.

Helft mir, ihr Schwes-tern, helft mir ver-scheu - chen ei - ne thö-rich-te
Help me, oh sis - ters, help me to ban - ish Fool__ ish fears that my

Ban - gig-keit; dass ich mit kla - rem Aug' ihn em-pfan - ge,
heart__ an-noy, That with un-cloud - ed eyes I may wel - come

streu - et ihm Blu - men, brin - get ihm knospen - de Ro - sen dar.
flow - ers be - fore him, Strew him fresh rose-buds with dain - ty art;

A - ber euch, Schwes-tern, grüss' ich mit Weh - muth, freu-dig schei-dend aus
Yet, oh my sis - ters, sad - ly I greet ye, Tho' in joy from your

eu - rer Schaar, freu-dig scheidend aus eu-rer Schaar.
band I part, tho' in joy from your band I part.

„Süsser Freund, du blickest."

"Sweet my friend, thou viewest."

(A. von Chamisso.)

English version by Dr. Th. Baker.

Composed 1840.
Op. 42, № 6.

Langsam, mit innigem Ausdruck.
Lento con affetto.

28.

Sü - sser Freund, du bli - ckest mich ver-
Sweet my friend, thou view - est me in

wun - dert an, kannst es nicht be - grei - fen, wie ich
fond a - maze, Canst not guess, why mine is now a

wei - nen kann; lass der feuch - ten Per - len un - ge - wohn - te Zier
tear - ful gaze? Let the rare a - dorn - ment, pearl - y drops, de - lay,

freu - dig hell er - zit - tern in dem Au - ge mir. Wie so
Glad - ly, bright - ly quiv - 'ring in mine eye to - day. How in

12873

bang mein Bu - sen, wie so won - ne - voll!   wüsst'__ ich
fear my bo - som, how in joy, doth swell!   *Had__ I*

nur mit Wor - ten, wie ich's sa - gen soll; komm und birg dein Ant - litz
words to tell thee what I fain would tell! Come and hide thy face, love,

hier an mei - ner Brust, will in's Ohr dir flü-stern al - le mei - ne Lust.
here up - on my breast, In thine ear I'll whis-per all my sweet un - rest.

Weisst du nun die
Now dost know the

12873

„An meinem Herzen, an meiner Brust."

"Here on my bosom, here on my heart."

(A. von Chamisso.)

English version by Dr. Th Baker.

Composed 1840.
Op. 42, N? 7.

Schneller. *Più mosso.*

nur ei - ne Mut - - ter weiss al - lein was
On - ly a moth - - er knows a - lone What

lie - ben heisst und glück - - lich sein.
bliss in love a heart may own.

O wie be-daur' ich doch den Mann, der
How pit - i-ful are men, I trow, Who

Mut - - ter-glück___ nicht füh - - len kann! Du
ne'er a moth - er's joys can know! Thou

„Nun hast du mir den ersten Schmerz gethan."

"Now for the first time thou hast giv'n me pain."

(A. von Chamisso.)

English version by Dr. Th. Baker.

Op. 42, Nº 8.
Composed 1840.

30.

Nun hast du mir den er-sten Schmerz ge-than, der a-ber
Now for the first time thou hast giv'n me pain, Ah, and so

traf. Du schläfst, du har-ter, un-barm-herz'-ger Mann, den To-des-
sore! Thou sleep-est, cru-el, un-com-pass'-nate man, To wake no

schlaf. Es bli-cket die Ver-lass'-ne vor sich hin, die Welt ist
more. Be-fore me, all for-sa-ken where I bow, The world's a

leer, ist leer. Ge-lie-bet hab' ich und ge-lebt, ich bin nicht
void, a void; I lov'd and liv'd for thee a-lone, and now My

le - bend mehr. Ich zieh'mich in mein Inn'-res still zu-rück, der
life's de-stroy'd. I si-lent-ly with-draw with-in my breast, The

Schlei - er fällt, da hab' ich dich und mein ver-lor-nes Glück, du mei-ne
veil doth fall; There I have thee and ev-'ry joy I lost, O thou, mine

Adagio.

Welt!
All!

Tempo wie das erste Lied.
(Larghetto.) Tempo as in the first song. (page 85)

Frühlingsfahrt.

Springtide Wandering.

(J. von Eichendorff.)

English version by Dr. Th. Baker.

Op. 45, Nº 2.
Composed 1840.

vol - len Früh-lings hin - aus._____
_bill - 'wy spring-tide, they roam._____

Die streb-ten nach ho - hen___ Din - gen, die
_Tho' fair or___ foul were the weath - er, The_

woll - ten, trotz Lust___ und Schmerz, was Rechts in der Welt voll -
tide in their hearts ran high, Their hope knew no bar-rier nor

brin - gen, und___ wem sie vor - ü - ber - gin - gen, dem___
_teth - er, And___ where they went by___ to - geth - er, There___

114

12873

116

12873

Früh - lingswohl ü - ber mir; und seh' ich so ke - cke Ge -
spring - tide roll o - ver me; At sight of such dar - ing young

ritard.

sel - - len, die Thrä - nen im Au - ge mir schwel - len_ach
fel - - lows, A tear in mine eye ev - er fol - - lows: O

ritard.

Langsamer.
Più lento.   *ritard.*

Gott, führ' uns lieb - reich zu dir,— ach Gott, führ' uns lieb - reich zu
Lord, lead us kind - ly to Thee!_ O Lord, lead us kind - ly to

ritard.

dir!
Thee!

ritard.

„Im wunderschönen Monat Mai."

In May.

(Heine.)

Composed 1840.
Op.48, № 1.

In wun - der - schö - nen Mo - nat Mai,   als
In May, the love - li - est of months,   *When*

al - le Knos-pen spran-gen,   da ist in mei - nem Her - zen   die
all the trees were bloom-ing, I felt with-in my bo - som Young

Lie - be auf - ge - gan - gen.
Lore his pow'r as - sum-ing.

ritar - dan - - do - -

p *a tempo*

Im wun - der-schönen Monat Mai, als al - le Vö - gel
'Twas in the love-li-est of'months, When all the birds were

a tempo

san - gen, da hab' ich ihr ge-stan - den mein Seh - nen und Ver-
sing - ing, I laid my heart be - fore her, My vows of true love

lan - gen.
bring-ing.

ri - tar - dan - do

Ped.

„Wenn ich in deine Augen seh'."

"Whene'er thine eyes I gaze upon."

(Heine.)

Composed 1840.
Op.48. Nº 4.

12873

ich mich lehn' an dei - ne Brust, kommt's ü - ber mich wie Him - mels-
I may lean up - on thy breast, *I* *feel a thrill of heav'n-ly*

Ped. ✻

ritard. a tempo

lust, doch wenn du sprichst: ich lie - be dich, so muss ich
zest; *But when thou say'st:* *"I love but thee," Then I must*

ritard.

a tempo

wei - nen bit - ter - lich.
weep most bit - ter - ly.

p

rit.

a tempo ritard.

pp

„Ich grolle nicht."
"I chide thee not."

English version by Dr. Th. Baker.

(Heine.)

Composed 1840.
Op. 48, N? 7.

„Und wüssten's die Blumen."

The broken heart.

(Heine.)

Composed 1840.
Op.48, № 8.

Und wüss - ten's die Blu-men, die klei - nen, wie
If on - ly the flow-ers could know it, How

tief ver-wun - det mein Herz, sie wür - den mit mir
deep - ly wound - ed my heart, They'd weep with me to

wei - nen, zu hei - len mei - nen Schmerz. Und
show it, With me, to heal the smart. The

wüss - ten's die Nach - ti - gal - len, wie ich so trau - rig und
night - in - gales, could they feel it, How ill my spir - it and

krank, sie lie - ssenfröh - lich er - schal - len er -
sore, They'd all be ry - ing to heal it With

qui - cken-den Ge - sang. Und wüss - ten sie mein
songs of sweet - est pow'r. If they but knew my

We - he, die gol - de-nen Ster - ne-lein, sie
an - guish, Yon stars in their bright ca - reer, They'd

„Hör' ich das Liedchen klingen."

"E'er when I hear them singing."

(Heine.)

English version by Dr. Th. Baker.

"Dichterliebe," Op. 48; № 10.
Composed 1840.

36.

Langsam.
Lento.

Hör' ich das Lied-chen klin-gen, das
E'er when I hear them sing-ing The

einst die Lieb - ste sang, so will mir die Brust zer-
song my sweet-heart sang, Wild long-ing a - ris - es,

sprin - gen von wil - dem Schmer - zens-drang. Es
wring-ing My breast with woe - ful pang. Then

treibt mich ein dunk - les Seh - nen hin - auf zur Wal - des -
drives me a name - less yearn - ing To yon - der wood on

höh, ___ dort löst sich auf ___ in Thrä - nen mein
high; ___ There melts my an - guish burn - ing While

ü - ber-grö - sses Weh.
tears o'er-flow mine eye.

ritard.

„Ich hab' im Traum geweinet."

"In dreams I fell a-weeping."

(Heine.)

English version by Dr. Th. Baker.

Composed 1840.
Op. 48, № 12.

„Allnächtlich im Traume:"

"In slumber I see thee nightly e'er:"

(Heine.)

English version by Dr. Th. Baker.

"Dichterliebe;" Op. 48; No 14.
Composed 1840.

38.

All-nächtlich im Traume seh' ich dich und se-he dich
In slumber I see thee night-ly e'er, And see thee so

freundlich, freund-lich grü-ssen, und laut aufweinend stürz'ich mich zu
kind-ly, kind-ly greet me; A-loud I sob, and fal-ling there Be-

dei-nen sü-ssen Fü-ssen.
fore thy feet pros-trate me.

Du sie-hest mich
Thou gaz-est on

an weh-mü-thig-lich und schüttelst, schüttelst das
me mourn-ful-ly now, And shak-est, shak-est thy

blon - de Köpfchen; aus   dei - nen Au - gen schleichen sich die   Per - len - thränen -
tress - es gleaming, While   pearl - y tears are gath'ring slow With - in thine eyes o'er-

ritard.   *a tempo*   *pp*

tröpfchen.   Du sagst mir   heimlich ein lei - ses
brimming.   *Thou whisp'rest soft - ly   a word a -*

ritard.   *a tempo*

Wort,   und giebst mir den Strauss,   den Strauss von Cy - pressen. Ich wa - che
non,   And giv'st me the cy - press-wreath for a   to-ken: Then I a -

auf,   und der Strauss ist fort, und's Wort hab' ich ver-ges-sen.
wake,   and the wreath is gone, And the word's as one un-spo-ken.

Die beiden Grenadiere.

The two Grenadiers.

(Heine.)

English version by Dr. Th. Baker.

Composed 1840.
Op.49, No. 1.

han - gen, da hör - ten sie bei - de die trau - ri - ge Mähr': dass
mourn-ing; For there they were met by the ti - dings of fear, That

Frank-reich ver - lo - ren ge - gan-gen, be - siegt und ge-schla - gen das
France in her pow - er was shak-en, De - feat - ed, de-stroy'd was the

tap - fe - re Heer und der Kai - ser, der Kai - ser ge - fan - gen.
ar - my so dear, And the Em-p'ror, the Em-p'ror was tak - en.

Da wein - ten zu-sammen die Gre-na-
Then wept they to-geth-er, the Gre-na-

dier' wohl ob der kläg - li - chen Kun - de; der Ei - ne
diers, To hear such news on re - turn - ing! And then one

wie-hern-der Ros - se Ge - tra - be;   dann rei - tet mein Kai - ser wohl
neigh of the charg-ers re - ply - ing.   *Then 'twill be the Em-p'ror that*

ü-ber mein Grab, viel Schwerter klir-ren und blit-zen,   viel Schwer-ter klir-ren und
rides o'er my grave, And swords are flashing and fall-ing,   *And swords are flashing and*

blit - zen: dann   steig' ich ge-waff-net her - vor aus dem Grab,   den
fall - ing!   *All*   *read - y and arm'd I'll a - rise from the grave,*   *The*

ritard.

Kai-ser, den Kai-ser zu schützen.
Emp'ror, the Emp'ror is call-ing!

Adagio.

ritard.

Volksliedchen.
Love-thoughts.

(Rückert.)

English version by Dr. Th. Baker.

Composed 1842.
Op 51, No 2.

Einfach.
Semplice.

40.

Wenn ich früh in den Gar - ten geh', in mei - nem grü - nen
When at morn in a dress of green I thro' the gar - den

Hut, ist mein er - ster Ge - dan - ke, was nun mein Lieb - ster
go, What I first think, I ween, Is: "How fares my true love

thut.
now?"

Am Him - mel steht kein
Were mine the stars on

Stern, den ich dem Freund nicht gönn - te, mein Herz gäb' ich ihm
high, There's none but he might have it, My heart I'd give, if

„Ich wand're nicht."
"I ne'er will roam."

(C. Christern.)

English version by Dr. Th. Baker.

Op. 51, No 3.
Composed 1840.

12873

Man singt in tau-send Wei-sen von Ber - gen, Fel-sen -
Al - lein, der Trank der Re - ben, er kommt ja auch hie -

They tell a thou-sand sto - ries Of moun - tains,rock - y
But here, when I com-mand it, The fin - est vin - tage

höh'n: al - lein wa-rum noch rei - sen, die Hei-math ist so
her, wo mir mein hol-des Le - ben ihn reicht, was will ich

heights, But why seek for-eign glo - ries, When home my heart de -
flows, And if my dear one hand it, I care not where it

schön, die Hei - math ist so schön!
mehr, was will, was will ich mehr?

lights, when home my heart de - lights?
grows, I care not where it grows!

Ich geh' nicht in's Ge - wim - mel
I will not seek for plea - sure

der gro - ssen, wei - ten Welt,
'Neath wid - er heav'ns be - yond,

den klar - sten, blau - sten
The clear - est, bright - est

Him - mel zeigt Lieb - chens Au - gen - zelt.
a - zure Is in her eye so fond.

Und mehr als Früh - lings - won - ne ver-
And more than spring-tide splen - dor Her

Auf dem Rhein.
On the Rhine.
(K Immermann.)

English version by Dr. Th. Baker.

Composed 1842.
Op. 51, No 4.

Ziemlich langsam.
Poco Adagio.

42.

Auf dei - nem Grun - de ha - ben sie an ver - borg' - nem
Far down in deeps of a - zure Thy wa - ters hold in

Ort den gold' - nen Schatz be - gra - - ben, der
ward, Well hid, a gold - en trea - - sure, The

Ni - be - lun - gen Hort. Ihn wah - ren dei - ne
Ni - be - lungs' rare hoard. With - in thy wave a -

Wel - len bis an den jüng - sten Tag, zu
bide it Un - til the Judg - ment Day, Where

Blondel's Lied.

Blondel's Song.

(Seidl.)

Composed 1840.
Op. 53, No 1.

Nicht schnell.
Moderato.

Spähend nach dem Ei - sen - git - ter
Gaz-ing on the i - ron grat-ing,

bei des Mon - des hel - lem Schein, steht ein Min - strel mit der Zi - ther
Where the gen - tle moon-beams fall, Stands a watch-ful min-strel wait-ing

vor dem Schlos - se Dür-renstein, stimmt sein Spiel zu sanfter Wei - se und beginnt sein
Near the cas - tle's pri-son-wall; Strikes the chords with soft e - mo - tion, Voice and lute in

Lied da - zu, denn ein Ah - nen sagt ihm lei - se: „su - che treu, so fin-dest du!"
skill com-bin'd, This the hope of his de - vo-tion, "Seek in faith, and thou wilt find!"

Kö - nig Ri - chard, Held von Os - ten,
Roy - al Rich - ard, li - on - heart - ed,

sankst du wirk - lich schon hin - ab? Muss dein Schwert im Mee - re ros - ten,
Rusts thy sword be - neath the wave? Or on earth has life de - part - ed,

o - der deckt dich fern ein Grab? Su - chend dich auf al - len We - gen
And thou moul - der'st in the grave? Far and wide in each di - rec - tion

wallt dein Min - strel oh - ne Ruh', denn ihm sagt ein lei - ses Re - gen:
Does thy min - strel cease-less wind, Prompted by the sweet re - flec - tion:

„su - che treu, so fin - dest du!"
"Seek in faith, and thou wilt find!"

Hof - fe, Ri - chard, und vertrau - e, Treu - e lenkt und lei - tet mich!
Hope, King Rich-ard, ing gai - ly, Trust - ful-ness has guid - ed me!

Und im fer-nen Hei - math-gau-e be - tet Lie - be still für dich!
From thy dis-tant lieg - es dai-ly Pray'rs of love a - rise for thee!

Blondel fol-get dei-nen Bah - nen, Margot winkt dir seh-nend zu, deinem Min-strel
Blondel fol-lows, per-se-ver - ing, Margot beck-ons, ill - resign'd; One glad thought my

sagt ein Ah-nen: „su-che treu, so fin-dest du!"
la-bor cheering, "Seek in faith, and thou wilt find!"

Horch, da tönt es lei - se, lei - se aus dem Burg-ver - liess _ her-vor,
Hark! what ten - der strains are flow-ing From the dun-geon · lone _ and drear?

ei - ne wohl - be - kann - te Wei - se klingt an Plon-del's lau - schend Ohr.
Wel-come, well-known mu - sic, throwing Joy on Blon-del's lis - t'ning ear.

Nach und nach schneller und stärker.
poco a poco accel. e crescendo.

Wie ein Freun-des - ruf, ein trau - ter, schallt sein ei - gen Lied ihm zu,
Like a friend's con - fid-ing mes-sage, Back his own song seems de-sign'd,

und sein Ah - nen sagt ihm lau - ter: „su - che treu, so fin - dest du!"
And he hails the joy-ful pre - sage, "Seek in faith, and thou wilt find!"

Heimwärts fliegt er mit der Kun-de, da war Leid und Freu-de gross, fliegt zurück mit
Home he flies, the land in rapture Hails the ti - dings he con-veys; He regains the

ed-ler Run-de, kauft den theu-ren Kö - nig los. Rings umstaunt vom fro-hen Kreise,
place of cap-ture, For the he - ro ran-som pays. 'Midst his cour-tiers' ac-cla-ma-tion,

stürzt der Held dem Sän-ger zu, gut bewährt hat sich die Wei-se, „su-che treu, so
In his arms the king entwin'd Him who caught the in-spi - ra-tion, "Seek in faith, and

fin-dest du!"
thou shalt find!"

Der arme Peter.

Poor Peter.

(Heine.)

Composed 1840.
Op. 53, № 3a, b, c.

I.

Nicht schnell.

44.

Der Hans und die Gre - te tan - zen her -
Smart John and his Marg' - ret dance with good

um, und jauch - zen vor lau - ter Freu - de, der
will, No hearts in the world are light - er; But

Pe - ter steht so still und so stumm, und ist so
Pe - ter stands so si - lent and still, His face than

blass wie Krei - de. Der Hans und die Gre - te sind
chalk seems whit - er. Smart John and fair Marg' - ret are

Etwas ruhiger.
un poco più moderato.

will's mich von hin - nen drän-gen. Es treibt mich nach der Lieb-sten Näh', als
This grief is al - ways press-ing: It drives me to my dar-ling's side, As

könnt's die Gre - te hei - len, doch wenn ich der in's Au - ge seh', muss
if her pow'r would heal it, But when with-in her eye I spied, I

Langsamer.
più lento.

ich von hin - nen ei - len. Ich steig' hin - auf des Ber - ges Höh',
nev - er dar'd re - veal it. I clam - ber up the moun - tain's height,

dort ist man doch al - lei - ne, und wenn ich
My - self a - lone there keep - ing, And when a -

Mäd-chen flü-stern sich ins Ohr: „der stieg wohl aus dem Grab her - vor!" Ach__
girls say in each oth - er's ear, "He doth from out the grave ap - pear!" A -

nein, ihr lie-ben Jung-fräu - lein, der steigt erst in das Grab hin - ein. Er
las! not so, ye maid - ens fair, This youth is swift-ly hast'ning there. His

hat ver-lo - ren sei-nen Schatz, drum ist das Grab der be-ste Platz, wo er am bes - ten
well-belov - ed he has lost; The grave is best for him that's cross'd, Where he his bones may

ritard.

lie-gen mag und schla-fen bis zum jüng-sten Tag!
gent-ly lay, And sleep un - til the judgment-day!

ritard.

pp

Die Soldatenbraut.

The Soldier's Bride.

(E. Mörike.)

English version by Dr. Th. Baker.

Composed 1847.
Op. 64, № 1.

Leicht, herzlich.
Leggero, sentito.

45.

Ach, wenn's nur der Kö-nig auch wüsst', wie wa-cker mein Schä-tze-lein ist! Für den Kö-nig da liess' er sein Blut, für mich a-ber e-ben-so gut, für mich a-ber e-ben-so gut. Mein

If on-ly the king, too, were told How true is my love, and how bold! For the king he would shed all his blood, For me just the same, so he would! For me just the same, so he would! My

poco ritard.   *a tempo*

Schatz hat kein' Band und kein Stern, kein Kreuz, wie die vor-neh-men
love has no rib-bon or star, *No cross, such as no-bles may*

Herrn, mein Schatz wird auch kein Ge-ne-ral:___ hätt' er
wear, *He'll nev-er be a gen-e-ral, I know,* *From the*

nur sei-nen Ab-schied ein-mal, hätt' er nur sei-nen Ab-schied ein-
ar-my I wish he could go! *from the ar-my I wish he could*

poco ritard. *a tempo*

Etwas langsamer.
Poco meno mosso.

mal! Es schei-nen drei Ster-ne so
go! *Three stars they are shin-ing so*

ritard.

hell ___ dort ü-ber Ma-ri-en-ca-pell'; da
bright, ___ *High o-ver the town thro' the night;* *Rose-*

12873

knüpft uns ein ro-sen-roth Band, ____ und ein Hauskreuz ist auch bei der
red shall a rib-bon there bind__ us, And in life__man-y cross-es shall

Hand.__
find us.

Erstes Tempo.
Tempo I.

Ach, wenn's nur der Kö - nig auch
If on - ly the king, too, were

wüsst', wie wa-cker mein Schä - tze - lein ist! Für den
told How true is my love, and how bold! For the

Kö - nig da liess' er sein Blut,— für mich a - ber e - ben - so
king he would shed all his blood, For me just the same, so he

gut, für mich a - ber e - ben - so gut,
would! For me just the same, so he would!

poco ritard. a tempo

für
For

mich a - ber e - ben - so gut._____
me just the same, so he would!_____

Aufträge.
Messages.

English version by Dr. Th. Baker.

(Ch. l'Égru.)

Op. 77, № 5.

46.

Sag', ich wä - re mit - ge - kom - men,
Say how fain I too were near - ing,

auf dir selbst her - ab ge - schwom - men:
On your wave a - down were steer - ing;

für den Gruss
'Stead of this

ei - nen Kuss kühn mir zu er -
For a kiss Bold - - ly then to

bit - ten; doch der Zeit Dring - lich - keit hätt' es nicht ge - lit -
sue her: But I may Not to - day Come my - self to woo

ten.
her!

Nicht so ei - lig! halt, er -
Not so hast - y, pray, de -

lau - be,
lay you,

klei - ne leicht be - schwing - te Tau - be!
Lit - tle light - ly - pin - ion'd fay, you!

Ha - be dir was auf - zu - tra - gen an die Lieb - ste
Here's a mes - sage you're to car - ry To my love be -

mein!
low!

Sollst ihr tau - send Grü - sse
Bear a thou - sand greet - ings:

sa - gen, hun - - - dert o - ben-drein!
mar - ry! Man - - - y more, I trow!

Sag', ich wär' mit dir ge-flo-gen,
Say, I fain like you were fly-ing,
ü - ber Berg und Strom ge-zo - gen:
O-ver hill and val - - ley hie - ing,

für den Gruss ei - nen Kuss kühn mir zu er -
'Stead of this For a kiss Bold - - ly then to

bit - ten; doch der Zeit Dring-lich - keit hätt' es nicht ge-lit -
sue her; But I may Not to day Come my-self to woo

ten.
her!
War-te nicht, dass ich dich trei-be,
Do not wait till I com-pel you,
o du
Oh you

trä - ge Mon - - des-schei - be!
la - zy moon, I tell you!
weiss's ja, was ich
You know well, what

dir be - foh - len für die Lieb-ste mein:
word you're bear - ing To my love be - low;
durch das
Thro' her

Fen - - ster-chen ver - stoh - len grü - - sse sie mir fein!
win - dow-pane in - peer-ing, Greet _____ her kind-ly now!

Marienwürmchen.
Ladybird.

English version by Dr. Th. Baker.

From "Des Knaben Wunderhorn."

Composed 1849.
Op. 79, № 14.

Nicht schnell.
Non allegro.

47.

Ma - ri - en - würm - chen, se - tze dich auf mei - ne Hand, auf
My La - dy - bird, come, light a - while up - on my hand, up -

mei - ne Hand, ich thu' dir nichts zu Lei - de, nichts, nichts zu
on my hand, You nev - er need to fear me, no, nev - er

Lei - de. Es soll dir nichts zu Leid gescheh'n, will nur dei - ne bun - ten
fear me; I will not harm you, pret - ty thing, On - ly let me see your

Flü - gel seh'n, bun - te Flü - gel mei - ne Freu - de!
gau - dy wing. Gau - dy wings I love so dear - ly!

12873

seh-re.
sad-ly.

Ma - ri - en-würm - chen, flie-ge hin zu
Now, La-dy-bird, fly— on to see Our

Nach-bars Kind, zu Nach-bars Kind, sie thun dir nichts zu Lei-de, nichts,
neigh-bors' child, our neigh-bors' child, Fly on, you need no warn-ing, you

nichts zu Lei-de. Es soll dir da kein Leid gescheh'n, sie wol-len dei - ne bun-ten
need no warning; They will not harm you, kind-ly things, They on-ly want to see your

Flü - gel seh'n, und grüss' sie al - le bei - de.
gau-dy wings; So bid them all good morning.

Abendlied.
Evening Song.

Composed 1842.
Op.85, N°12.

geh' zur Ruh' _____ auch du, mein mü - des Herz, der
sleep thou too, _____ *Thou too, my wea - ry heart.* *Soft*

A - bend-wind säu - selt lind, schlaf ein, schlaf ein, der Tag geht nun zur Ruh, nun zur
sighs the breeze through the trees, sleep on, sleep on, Since day to rest with-drew, day with-

Ruh', _____ nun zur Ruh', nun schlaf auch du! Und la - gert Dun - kel
drew, _____ day with - drew, Now sleep — thou too. Tho' dark-ness hangs o'er

nun auf Flur und Feld, ein mil - des Leuch - ten fliesst vom Himmels-zelt,
for-est, field, and stream, The vault of heav'n now smiles with gen-tle beam,

der Mond aus Wol - ken - schlei - ern giesst hel - len Schein, giesst hel-len Schein.
Through clouds of flee - cy light-ness Bright shines the moon, bright shines the moon.

12873

Die Tochter Jephta's.
Jephtha's Daughter.
(Byron.)

Composed 1849.
Op.95, №1.

Mit Affect. (♩= 126.)
Con affetto.

umph kam durch mich euch her-bei,
won the great bat - - tle for thee,

und mein Va – – ter, die Hei – – math, sind
And my fa - - ther and coun - - try are

frei! _____
free! _____

Wenn das Blut, das du
When the blood of thy

gabst, ist ent-wallt,
giv - - ing hath gush'd,

die du
When the

An den Mond.

"Sun of the sleepless."

(Byron.)

Composed 1849.
Op.95. № 2.

50.

Langsam.
Lento.

Schlaf - lo - ser Son - ne, me - lan - chol' - scher Stern! Dein
Sun of the sleep - less! mel - an - chol - y star! Whose

thrä - nen - vol - ler Strahl er - zit - tert
tear - ful beam glows trem - u - lous - ly

fern, du of - fen - barst die Nacht, die dir nicht
far, That show'st the dark - ness thou canst not dis-

Dem Helden.
The Hero.

(Byron.)

Composed 1849.
Op.95, No.3.

Mit Begeisterung. (♩= 72.)
Con entusiasmo.

51.

Dein Tag ist aus, dein Ruhm fing
Thy days are done, thy fame be-

an, es preist des Volks Ge - sang dich, Ho - her, auf des
gun; Thy coun - try's strains re - cord The tri - umphs of her

Sie - - - ges Bahn, dein Schwert im
cho - - - son son, The slaugh - - ters

Fein - - des - drang, die Tha - ten all', die
of his sword! The deeds he did, the

„Kennst du das Land?"
"Know'st thou the land?"

English version by Dr. Th. Baker.

(Goethe.)

Composed 1849.
Op.98, N⁰1.

Langsam, die beiden letzten Verse mit gesteigertem Ausdruck. (♪ = 69.)
Lento. (*the last two verses with intensified expression*).

p

52.

p

Kennst du das
Know'st thou the

Land wo die Zi - tro - nen blüh'n? im dun - klen Laub die Gold - o - ran - gen glüh'n,
land where-in the lem - on blooms? The gold - en or - ange glows in leaf - y glooms,

Ped.   *   Ped.   *   Ped.   *

cresc.

in sanf - - ter Wind vom blau - - en Him - mel weht, die
From a - zure skies soft breez - - es gen - tly lave The

3   3   3   3   cresc.   fp   fp

fp   cresc.

Myr-the still,   und   hoch   der   Lor - beer steht; kennst   du   es
myr - tle hushed, and   high   the   lau - rels wave; Know'st   thou it

fp   fp   cresc.

Ped.   *   Ped.

12873

„Dein Angesicht."

"Thy lovely face, so dear to me."

(Heine.)

Composed 1850–51.
Op.127, No.2.

bleich der Tod, ____ er - lö - schen wird das Him - mels - licht, das
pale and cold, ____ And soon the heav'n - ly light will die That

aus den from - men Au - gen bricht. Dein An - ge - sicht, so
beams so bright-ly in thine eye. Thy love - - ly face, so

lieb und schön, das hab' ich jüngst im Traum ___ ge - seh'n: es
dear to me, I seem'd one night in dreams ___ to see: It

ist so mild und en - gel - gleich, und doch so bleich, so schmer - - zen -
is so mild, an - gel - i - cal, And yet so pale, so sor - - row -

reich.
ful.

12873

Schlusslied des Narren.
Clown's Song.
(Shakespeare.)

German transl. (v. 1 and 2) by
A.W. von Schlegel.

Composed 1850-51.
Op.127, No 5.

Lebhaft.
Vivace.

54.

Und als ich ein win-zig Büb-chen war, hop
When that I was a lit-tle boy, With

hei-sa, hop hei-sa, bei Re-gen und Wind, da mach-ten zwei-e nun e-ben ein Paar, denn der
hey, ho, with hey, ho, the wind and the rain, A fool-ish thing was but a toy, For the

Re-gen, der reg-net jeg-li-chen Tag. Und als ich, ach, ein Weib that frein, hop
rain it rain-eth ev-er-y day. But when I came to man's e-state, With

a tempo

hei-sa, hop hei-sa, bei Re-gen und Wind, da woll-te mir Müs-sig-
hey, ho, with hey, ho, the wind and the rain, 'Gainst knaves and thieves men

Romanze.

English version by Dr. Th. Baker.

Romance.

(Poem by E. Geibel, after the Spanish.)

Nicht schnell.
Non allegro.

Composed 1849.
Op. 138, N⁰5.

55.

12873